Power Tools Part 2: Worship Power

Building Foundations: A Spirit Filled Children's Church Curriculum

Pastor Tamera Kraft
Revival Fire 4 Kids Resource

Mt Zion Ridge Press
http://mtzionridgepress.com
Managing Editors: Michelle L. Levigne and Tamera Lynn Kraft
Cover Art: Tamera Lynn Kraft

ISBN: 978-1-955838-10-8

Registration and Digital Files (Available for FREE with purchase of the curriculum): Digital files (jpeg graphics, video clips, other resources) are available to anyone who purchases and registers this curriculum at no additional cost. To register, click on this link http://eepurl.com/glsELH or type it in the address box on your browser and fill out the form. We never sell or give away any information we receive.

DVD: If you prefer a DVD of Jpeg images and video clips, you may purchase it at http://mtzionridgepress.com for an additional cost.

Power Tools is a 3 part curriculum which includes these sections that can be bought together in one manual or bought separately:

- Part 1 – Prayer Power (4 lessons on the power of prayer)
- **Part 2 – Worship Power (4 Lessons on the power of worshipping God included in this manual)**
- Part 3 – Holy Spirit Power (5 lessons on how the baptism and gifts of the Holy Spirit equip you with power)

Power Tools is available in PDF download and print. Each part of *Power Tools* is available separately in PDF download or print.

All Scripture in this curriculum is from the NIV (2011) Bible unless otherwise designated.

THE HOLY BIBLE, NEW INTERNATIONAL VERSION®, NIV® Copyright © 1973, 1978, 1984, 2011 by Biblica, Inc.® Used by permission. All rights reserved worldwide.

Some Scripture is also used from these versions:

THE HOLY BIBLE, INTERNATIONAL CHILDREN'S BIBLE® ICB Copyright© 1986, 1988, 1999, 2015 by Tommy Nelson™, a division of Thomas Nelson. Thomas Nelson is a registered trademark of HarperCollins Christian Publishing, Inc.

NEW KING JAMES VERSION® NKJV® Scripture taken from the New King James Version®. Copyright © 1982 by Thomas Nelson. Used by permission. All rights reserved.

For questions about copyright issues or other matter concerning rights for this curriculum, contact revivalfire4kids@att.net.

Building Foundations Curriculum is a Revival Fire for Kids resource. For more information about Revival Fire for Kids, check out their website at http://revivalfire4kids.net

Materials included:

Worship Power: 4 complete downloadable lessons including 8 object lessons, 8 skits, 8 games, 4 Bible Stories, 8

Worship Expression Lessons, 4 memory verse activities, graphics to be used in PowerPoint slides for 4 lessons, 4 small group discussions, and optional lessons and activities. Lessons, graphics, videos, and Family Devotion Handouts will be available for immediate download.

Table of Contents

How To Use This Curriculum:

Scriptural Premise: God does not leave us powerless in our Christian journey. He gives us tools to empower us for everything He wants us to do. Among these power tools are prayer, worship, the baptism of the Holy Spirit, and the gifts of the Holy Spirit.

Decorations: Decorations and set design should reflect building construction with drills, saws, and power tools. If you have purchased *The Journey*, another *Building Foundations Curriculum*, you could use the decorations for *The Journey* and add power tools. You could also borrow power tools from someone and set up a power tools garage or store.

Another idea is to use a backdrop with the cover picture of *Power Tools* or Power Tools backdrop as templates for a backdrop. You can use any image included with this curriculum by projecting the image using a video projector onto a box or backdrop and drawing it. Use your creativity.

Italics: Italics are used for Scripture. They are also used in this curriculum for passages or speeches the teacher or worker may want to say in their own words. For skits, italics are only used to designate the person speaking.

Welcome:

Welcome: Each lesson will welcome the children with an introduction to that day's message.

Prayer: It's important to start each lesson with prayer.

Rules: A list of 5 Ups are included in the graphics available after registration. Rehearse the rules every week.

Theme Song: Get the kids up and moving at the beginning of every lesson with a fun theme song. Theme songs that will work with this curriculum are *We Love Jesus* by High Voltage Kids, *Shout* by Yancy, *or Open the Heavens* by Gateway Kids.

Memory Verse: Every lesson has a memory verse. The verse will be included in a slide and will be illustrated in three ways. You can choose to use any of these illustrations to teach the verse, or you could use all three throughout your lesson.

Memory Verse Skit: A puppet or live skit with Doctor Word is included in each lesson to introduce the Memory Verse. The person doing the skit can dress as a doctor or in scrubs. If a doctor, nurse, or medical professional attends you church, it would be great to him for your skits and have him wear his work clothes. You can also use a doctor puppet for these skits if you have a puppet team.

Memory Verse Talk: This is a short talk explaining what the verse means to the children. Memorizing God's Word is important, but it's more important for your students to know what a verse means.

Memory Verse Activity: Children learn by seeing, reading, hearing, and doing. The memory verse activity is a simple tool to help students remember the verse longer.

Game Time: A Game Time slide is included with registration for this curriculum. It isn't necessary to include a game with every week's lesson, but if you do, you should have a fun game that relates to the lessons. Game Time is the place for that. You may also want to save the game for last so, if the adult service runs long, you can play games until the parents arrive to retrieve their children.

Video Clips: *Power Tools Countdown* and video clips for some lessons are included with *Worship Power* along with other downloadable files. A link to a Dropbox files with be sent to your email after you have registered your curriculum. *Building Foundations* doesn't provide video curriculum to teach the lessons. Instead, it provides short, fun video clips to help the children remember the lesson in a fun way.

Offering: Lessons include a short talk on why children should give in the offering. You can expand the fun by having an offering contest with the boys against the girls. You can use a scale with buckets or have two offering plates and count the money. Once a month or once a quarter, have a special reward for the winning team.

Praise & Worship: Each week, a time of praise and worship is included to ready the students' hearts to hear the Word of God. This curriculum does not provide music because every church has different musical needs.

Lesson of the Week:

Skit: Two skits about each week's lesson are included. One skit uses a doctor, Doctor Word, to introduce the memory verse for the day. Another skit uses a silly character named Tyler the Power Tool Guy or Gal. These skits require few props and only two people, the leader and another worker, making them easy for even small churches to use. Doctor Word skits can be used as puppet skits if you have a puppet ministry. Tyler the Power Tool Guy or Gal could also be used with puppets but may need some modification when props are involved.

Bible Story: Each week, a Bible story is included to go with the lesson.

Object Lessons: At least two object lessons illustrate the points of each week's lesson. Resources for the object lessons are not included.

Worship Expressions: At least two worship or praise words will be taught each lesson with a Bible story or activity and verse to go with them.

Message: A short message ties up the lesson for the day and asks for a response from the students.

Optional Resources: Optional Resources are included with object lessons and other interactive events as suggestions for additional teaching activities. The props for optional resources are not included but are easy to obtain.

Small Group Chat/Activity: Some children's ministries prefer to end each children's service with a small group chat, or they have a small group Bible study at some time during the week. Small group chat questions and activities are included for these purposes. Divide students into small groups of not more than six children. You can divide them by ages or include different ages together. Questions and instructions for activities are included to help the leader facilitate a chat with the students about the lesson. Small group sessions will help your students go home with practical applications for what they have learned.

Home Application: Each lesson will include a handout for the children to take home. Each handout will include this week's memory verse, a summary of the lesson, a Bible reading for each day, and a weekly family activity. This handout is available as a printable PDF download upon registration of this curriculum. This will be helpful guide for parents who have family devotions.

Registration and Digital Files (Available for FREE with purchase of the curriculum): Digital files (jpeg graphics, video clips, other resources) are available to anyone who purchases and registers this curriculum at no additional cost. To register, click on this link http://eepurl.com/glsELH or type it in the address box on your browser and fill out the form. We never sell or give away any information we receive.

Power of Worship

Created to Worship

Luke 4:8 (NIV) *...Worship the Lord your God. He is the only one you should serve.*

Worthy of Worship

Psalm 29:2 (NKJV) *Give unto the Lord the glory due to His name; Worship the Lord in the beauty of holiness.*

Worship in Spirit and in Truth

John 4:24 (NKJV) *God is Spirit, and those who worship Him must worship in spirit and truth.*

Enjoying Worship

Psalm 16:11 (NKJV) *You will show me the path of life; In Your presence is fullness of joy; At Your right hand are pleasures forevermore.*

Lesson 1 – Created to Worship

Focus Point: The reason we were created is to worship God.

Goal: Because we were created to worship God, we can only find true satisfaction in Him.

Verse of the Day: Luke 4:8 (NIV) ...*Worship the Lord your God. He is the only one you should serve.*

Supplies Needed:

- doctor puppet or doctor costume for skit
- portable toolbox with various tools
- Tyler the Power Tool Guy Skit: Tyler wears a portable toolbox or toolbelt with various tools and is dressed in blue jeans and a plaid shirt, etc.
- 2 spoons
- 2 hard boiled eggs or tennis balls
- obstacles (optional)
- a variety of power tools (optional - manual tools)
- marker board, chalk board, or blank wall
- scotch tape
- colored sheets of paper
- perfume or spikenard essential oil
- cup
- bottle or pitcher of water
- Lego block or toy house

Opening: *Power Tools Countdown* or *Power Tools* Slide (Available free with registration of this curriculum.)

Welcome: *Welcome to Worship Power, part 2 of Power Tools. For the next few weeks, we will learn about one of the most powerful tools in a Christian's life, the power of worship. We were all created by God to worship Him. That is our primary purpose in life, and we can never truly be satisfied unless we worship God. Worship is something that flows out of us as we encounter God. The more we know God, the more we will want to worship Him, and the more we worship Him, the more we will know God.*

There's no better time to worship God than now. When I say go, for five minutes, let's tell God how worthy He is. You can shout Hallelujah or say you're worthy, or even I love you, Jesus or Praise the Lord..

Tell the students when to start. If your students are not ready for five minutes, start them out at one minute, and build from there.

Prayer: Ask a child to pray over the service.

Rules: (use rules slide) Go over the 5 Ups Rules.

Go over the *5 Ups Rules*: 1. Sit up straight. 2. Listen up. 3. Hush up. 4. Don't get up and run around or go to the bathroom. 5. Worship Up! (stand up and participate during praise and worship)

Theme or Activity Songs: Choose one of two fast moving activity or theme songs that go with the curriculum.

Game Time: Wacky Spoon Race (use game time slide)

Supplies Needed: 2 spoons, 2 hard boiled eggs or tennis balls, obstacles (optional)

What are spoons created for? Allow students to answer. *What are eggs (ping pong balls) created for?* Allow students to answer. *What are people created for?* Allow students to answer. *People can do a lot of things, but the reason they are created is to worship God. Today, we're going to use these spoons and eggs (ping pong balls) for a purpose they aren't created for.*

Have two teams do a relay race. The first student on each team has to balance an egg or ping pong ball on his spoon and run the relay race. You can use obstacles to make the race harder. Then, they have to run the race back to home base and give the spoon and egg (ping pong balls) to the next player in the line. If a student drops his egg or ball, he has to go back to the beginning. For younger students, the student can pick up the egg (ping pong ball) and continue from where he dropped it. Students can't use their other hands to touch, hold, or steady the egg (ping pong ball).

The team that has all the players run the race first wins.

Memory Verse Skit: (use Worship Power Lesson 1, slide A)

Supplies needed: doctor puppet or doctor costume for skit

Doctor Word: Hi kids. I'm Doctor Word. I'm called that because I'm a doctor and because I love the Word of God. The heart is only about the size of a fist, but it's a very important tool in the human body. The purpose of the heart is to pump blood through the network of blood vessels called the arteries and veins. This blood carries nutrients and oxygen throughout the body. If the heart stops beating, the nutrients and oxygen have no way to get to the other parts of the body, and the person dies.

Everyone of us was created for a purpose. That purpose is to worship God. If we don't carry out our purpose, our spiritual life suffers and eventually dies. That's why today's memory verse is so important. Luke 4:8b (NIV) says *...Worship the Lord your God. He is the only one you should serve.*

Remember, worship is as important to your spiritual life as your heart is to your body. Worship is powerful.

Offering: Worship in Giving

(Mark 12:41-44)

Did you know offering is an act of worship? In the book of Mark, Jesus watched people giving their offering. Some rich people gave a lot in the offering, but a poor widow only gave a little bit. That's because she gave everything she had. Jesus told the disciples that she'd given the most because she gave everything. She loved God, and so she worshipped God by giving all she had.

Skit: Tyler the Power Tool Guy and His Power Tools

Supplies Needed: Tyler has a portable toolbox or toolbelt with various tools and is dressed in blue jeans and a plaid shirt, etc., a variety of power tools (If you don't have power tools, manual tools will do.) If you use a girl in the skit, have her dress the same and call her Tyler the Power Tool Gal.

(Tyler, the Power Tool Guy, comes into the room. All his tools are laid out on a table in the front.)

Leader: Tyler, the Power Tool Guy. I'm so glad you could come today.

Tyler the Power Tool Guy: You said you needed me. What happened? Do you have an outlet that needs replaced? Or maybe you had the roof collapse, and you need it fixed? That would be dangerous, you know. Or did you need me to build something? I have a lot of power tools. Just let me know what you need, and I'll build it for you.

Leader: Thanks, Tyler. I knew you'd want to help me, but I don't need anything built, fixed, or replaced.

Tyler: I don't understand. Why did you ask me to bring all my tools?

Leader: Today, we're teaching the children they were created to worship God. Everyone and everything have a purpose. I was wondering if you could explain the purpose of some of your tools.

Tyler: I'd love to. (Adlib here. Have Tyler show the student each tool on the table and tell what its purpose is.)

Leader: Thanks, Tyler. I appreciate you telling the children the purpose for each of these tools.

Tyler: No problem. I'm glad to do it. But there's something I don't understand.

Leader: What's that, Tyler.

Tyler: You said that the main purpose we were created for is to worship God. I thought my purpose in life was to repair things and to tell people about Jesus.

Leader: I have a couple of questions for you. Why do you tell others about Jesus? And why do you repair things?

Tyler: Those questions are easy. I tell other about Jesus because I love Him and I want people to know how wonderful He is. I repair things because God gave me an ability to do that, and I want to honor Him by doing a good job.

Leader: So, you love God, and because of that you tell others about Him and honor Him by doing the things He's called you to do?

Tyler: That's right.

Leader: In other words, you honor and worship God by telling other about Him and by repairing things.

Tyler: How about that? You're absolutely right. When I do the things God wants me to do, it's because I love Him and want to worship and honor Him.

Leader: See, Tyler. Your main purpose in life is to worship God. When you do that, everything else you do is to honor and serve Him. You were created to worship.

(Tyler exits)

Verse of the Day: Luke 4:8 (NIV) ...*Worship the Lord your God. He is the only one you should serve.*

Memory Verse Talk: (use Worship Power Lesson 1, slide A)

Have your students repeat the memory verse several times. *We were all created to worship God, but did you know that every person, whether he loves God or rejects Jesus as his Savior will worship Jesus. Even Satan will worship Jesus one day. Philippians 2:9-11 (NIV) says, "Therefore God exalted him to the highest place and gave him the name that is above every name, that at the name of Jesus every knee should bow, in heaven and on earth and under the earth, and every tongue acknowledge that Jesus Christ is Lord, to the glory of God the Father.*

We have a choice for now. We can worship Jesus and receive great satisfaction in doing what we were created to do, or we can refuse. But those who choose not to worship Jesus will one day have no choice. They will have to bow their knees and worship Him, but they won't getting any blessing or satisfaction from doing so.

I want to worship Jesus now, knowing that when I worship Him, I'm doing what I was created to do.

Memory Verse Activity: Memory Verse Chairs

Supplies needed: marker board, chalk board, or blank wall; scotch tape, colored sheets of paper (each sheet has one word of the memory verse on it)

Preparation: Tape the sheets of paper on the bottom of random chair the students will be sitting on.

Let the students know, the words of the memory verse are taped to their chairs. When you say go, the students will look under their seats and find the words. Then they tape them to the marker board or wall in order.

If you have enough students, have teams with different colors and make one set of words in each color.

Bible Story: Mary's Act of Worship

(John 12:1-8)

Supplies needed: perfume or spikenard essential oil

This is perfume (spikenard). Expensive perfume can cost a lot of money, but it sure smell good.

Spray perfume or dab on some spikenard so your students can smell it.

The most expensive perfume in the world is called Shumukh by Spirit of Dubai. It costs $1.295 million an ounce. I bet that perfume really smells good.

Good perfume has always been expensive. In Bible days, young women who could afford it would buy expensive perfume in an alabaster box made of marble. The only way to open the box to allow the scent of the perfume out was to break it. A woman would save the perfume box and break it on her wedding night so her husband could share the scent of the perfume with her.

This story is about a young woman named Mary who had an alabaster box of spikenard, an expensive perfume for that day. Her brother, Lazarus, had invited Jesus over for dinner. Mary loved her brother, Lazarus, and her sister, Martha. Earlier that week, Lazarus had died. Mary cried a lot when that happened, but Jesus brought Lazarus back to life. Mary was so grateful. She knew Jesus is the Son of God, and as much as she loved her brother and sister, she loved Jesus even more. She wanted to worship Him and show Him how much she loved Him.

Lazarus invited Jesus to his home, and Martha was cooking and serving dinner. Mary wanted to do something special for Jesus too. At some point, she remembered her alabaster box of spikenard perfume. No doubt, she had spent a lot of money on that perfume and was saving it for her wedding. That was the best way she could think of to worship Jesus.

She broke the alabaster box and poured it on Jesus' feet. Then she wiped his feet with her long hair. The beautiful fragrance of spikenard filled the room. The worship Mary had poured out smelled so good.

But one of Jesus' disciples was indignant. He told Jesus that what Mary did, pouring out that expensive perfume, was wrong and wasteful. She could have at least sold the perfume and given the money to the poor. Mary must have felt awful when Judas said that. She was just trying to pour out her love and worship on Jesus. Maybe she should have sold the perfume. She could have shown Jesus her love by feeding the poor.

Jesus shouted at Judas, "Leave her alone. She has done a beautiful thing."

Mary was so happy to hear Jesus say that. He understood that all she wanted to do was worship Him. Even the perfume she poured out wasn't as valuable to her as Jesus was.

Mary poured out extravagant worship on Jesus. God wants us to do the same. He wants us to pour out extravagant worship every time we worship Jesus. It's what He created us to do. When we worship Him, we feel satisfied in a way nothing else can satisfy because we are doing what God wants us to do, we are giving God glory.

Worship Expression: Tehillah (Use Power Worship Lesson 1, slide B)

Tehillah is a word that means to praise God with singing. That's why we sing songs every service. It's one way to worship and praise God. Psalm 149:1 (NIV) says, "Praise the Lord. Sing to the Lord a new song, his praise in the assembly of his faithful people." We're about to sing some songs, but we're not singing because it's something we always do in church or even because we like singing. Singing songs to God is one way of worshipping Him. As we sing today, let's think about the words as we sing our songs to God.

Praise and Worship: Choose a couple of fast song and a slow song to lead children into praise and worship. It works well to talk to the children about what worship is and why it's important before you enter into this time. You can have a children's praise team, but until they understand leading praise and worship, have an adult leader or yourself be the worship leader.

Video: Why Worship

Use Worship Power downloadable video, Why Worship, for Power Tools downloadable resources.

Object Lessons:

1. The Purpose of a Cup

Supplies needed: cup, bottle or pitcher of water

Show the students your cup. *Why do you think this cup was created?* Allow students to answer. Pour water into the cup and drink out of it. *This cup was created to drink fluid out of. What are some other things we can use this cup for even though it wasn't created for those things?* Allow students to answer. If they have trouble, make suggestions.

The reason we can use this cup for other things is because of the shape of the cup. It's easy to use the cup to drink from because it's shaped to hold liquid, and that means it can be used for those other things as well.

We are created to worship God. Because God made us to worship, we can do other things. Different people have different talents and gifts. They can use those talents and gift to honor God. Sometimes we tell our friends about Jesus and invite Him to church. We do that because we love and worship God and want our friends to love God too. It is an expression of worship. Sometimes people like to learn about science, math, or history, or they like to read a lot. The more we learn about God's creation, the more we can worship Him for what He's created. Some people work at jobs where they make lots of money. They can use that money to give an offering to worship God.

Whatever we do, we can do it unto the Lord. In other words, we were created to worship God in everything we do and are. The reverse is also true.

Pick up the cup. *I can refuse to drink out of this cup. I can throw it in the trash, so nobody will ever drink out of it again. Or I can poke holes in it so even if I do fill it with water, the water will leak out. That still doesn't change the fact that it is a cup.*

I was created to worship God, but I can refuse to worship God. I can say I don't believe in God or that I do believe in Him, but I don't want to worship Him. The problem is I was still created to be a worshipper, and I still will worship, but I'll worship other things. The Bible calls those things idols. Idols aren't just weird statues people in Bible times used to worship. An idol is anything we worship instead of God.

We can worship God with our money, or we can worship our money. We can worship God with our gifts and talents, or we can worship our gifts and talents. We can learn more about the world we live in and worship God for creating it, or we can worship math or science or the other things we study. We can worship God by telling our friends about Him, or we can worship our friends by doing things with them that we shouldn't be doing. Even something as simple as baseball or video games can become an idol if we put it before God. We were created to worship God not idols.

2. God Lives in Our Worship (Use Worship Power Lesson 1, slide C)

Supplies needed: Lego block or toy house

God has promised He will always be with Him, and that's true. God is everywhere at the same time, so He is always with us. But sometimes, we sense God's presence. We may feel a strange warmth or peace. Sometimes adults will say, "God is here." Of course, God is everywhere, but they mean they sense His presence. Many times, this happens when we are focused on God, when we pray, or when we are reading or listening to God's Word. Sometimes it even happens when we aren't doing any of those things.

Then there are times when the Manifest Presence of God shows up. The word, manifest, in the Bible means to uncover or make apparent. When we talk about the Manifest Presence of God, we're talking about uncovering and making apparent the Glory of God. When God's Glory is uncovered, a lot of things might happen. The Bible talks about people falling to the ground because they couldn't stand in the presence of God. This is sometimes called being slain in the Spirit.

In the book of Acts, the Bible describes people being so filled with the Holy Spirit and with joy and laughter, they appear drunk. Sometimes people fall on their knees or faces or take their shoes off. Sometimes they shout, and sing, and dance before the Lord. Sometimes people get very quiet. All of those things are the result of the Manifest Presence of God, but I'm going to talk about something that brings about the Manifest presence of God.

Show and read slide C. *Psalm 22:3 says, "But You are holy, enthroned in the praises of Israel." This verse says God is enthroned in the praise of His people. God sits on His throne in Heaven. Another word for His throne is His dwelling place or His house.*

Show Lego house. *When we worship God, God lives in our worship. His throne sits in our worship. That's why so many amazing things happen when we really decide to worship God with everything within us. Our worship is where God's glory lives. When we worship Him, He shows up and reveals Himself or uncovers Himself to us. Wow, no wonder worshipping God satisfies us like nothing else can.*

Message: Our Worship Shows Our Love (Use Power Worship Lesson 1, slide D)

Supplies Needed: none

Show slide D. *One reason worship is so important to God is because it is the way we show God how much we love Him. In Matthew 22:37, "Jesus replied, 'Love the Lord your God with all your heart and with all your soul and with all your mind.'"*

Someday, when you grow up, you might find someone you want to marry and spend the rest of your life with. When that happens, you'll want to express your love for that person. You might want to buy that person gifts or show affection by kissing or hugging. There are lots of ways to express love to the person you marry.

There are also lots of ways to express our love for God. We'll be learning more about these expressions of worship over the next few weeks. We've already learned how we can express our love to God by singing. I'm going to tell you a few other ways, and I want you all to act out the ways I tell you.

Have the children do each of these actions: kneeling, lying on the floor face up or face down, shouting hallelujah or Jesus, raising your hands, being very silent, spinning around, dancing.

Response Time:

Talk to the students about expressing their worship for God using one of these ways. Explain that you will play music and then lay your hand on each of their heads while they are worshipping. They should continue to worship while you're doing this and after you stop. Make sure you have a catcher for any students who might not be able to stand during worship.

Because God loves it when we express out love, He lives in our worship and makes us satisfied and joyful in Him. Some things might happen. You might feel so woozy you can't stand up. If that happens, our helper will stand behind you and gently lower you to the floor. Some of you might cry, but they will be tears that make you feel better. Some might laugh because God makes you so happy. Some of you might just stand, kneel, or sit while God fills you with His peace and love.

Whatever way, God shows Himself to you, don't rush it. Keep worshipping Him and staying in His manifest presence.

During response time, allow the Holy Spirit to lead you. Lay hands on the students as you see them respond to the Holy Spirit. Don't worry about saying the right thing or praying a long prayer. You can say simple phrases like "fill" or "more Lord." Keep your hand gently on each student's head until you feel led to go to the next student.

Small Group Activity: Debrief

Supplies needed: none

Spend some time talking to your students about what happened during worship time. Tell them about some of your past experiences worshipping God.

Lesson 2 – Worthy of Worship

Focus Point: We worship God because He is worthy of worship.

Goal: Students will learn that only God is worthy of our worship.

Verse of the Day: Psalm 29:2 (NKJV) *Give unto the Lord the glory due to His name; Worship the Lord in the beauty of holiness.*

Supplies Needed:

- doctor puppet or doctor costume for skit
- portable toolbox with various tools
- Tyler the Power Tool Guy Skit: Tyler wears a portable toolbox or toolbelt with various tools and is dressed in blue jeans and a plaid shirt, etc.
- toys, candy, and prizes
- story bag or tote bag
- stuffed animal sheep
- plant or picture of a bush
- flash paper (optional)
- lighter
- fake chains or picture of slave in chains
- name tag with I AM written on it
- name tag with YAHWEH written on it
- slice of bread
- flashlight
- Lego block door
- jar or glass
- pebbles
- sand
- pitcher of water

Opening: *Power Tools Countdown* (optional) or *Power Tools* Slide

Welcome: Worthy of Worship

Welcome children. Only God is worthy of worship, so let's start today's service with some praise and worship. For five minutes, let's tell God how worthy He is. You can shout Hallelujah or say you're worthy, or even I love you, Jesus.

Tell the students when to start. If your students are not ready for five minutes, start them out at one minute, and build from there.

Prayer: Ask a child to pray over the service.

Rules: (use rules slide) Go over the 5 Ups Rules.

Go over the *5 Ups Rules*: 1. Sit up straight. 2. Listen up. 3. Hush up. 4. Don't get up and run around or go to the bathroom. 5. Worship Up! (stand up and participate during praise and worship)

Theme or Activity Songs: Choose one of two fast moving activity or theme songs that go with the curriculum.

Game Time: Treasure Hunt (use game time slide)

Supplies needed: toys, candy, and prizes hidden around the room

Tell the students there are treasures hidden in the room. Let them know if there are any places they can't look. When you say go, they have five minutes to find all the prizes. You can let them know how many are hidden if you want. When the time is up, it's nice to have some extra small prizes for students who haven't found any.

As hard as you looked for some of these prizes, God is an even greater treasure we can seek by worshipping Him. Matthew 13:44 (NIV) says, "The kingdom of heaven is like treasure hidden in a field. When a man found it, he hid it again, and then in his joy went and sold all he had and bought that field."

Memory Verse Skit: (use Worship Power Lesson 2, slide A)

Supplies needed: doctor puppet or doctor costume for skit

Doctor Word: Hi kids. I'm Doctor Word. To become a doctor, I had to go to school for eight years. Then I took a difficult test to prove I knew everything I needed to know about medicine. You would think after all that, I would be a full-fledged doctor, but I had to become a resident and learn a specialty for three years. Some specialties take as long as six years. All the time and work was worth it because I became worthy to be called a doctor and a surgeon. Just think about it. God is the only being worthy of our praise and worship, not because He went to God school, but because He is that great. Psalm 29:2 (NKJV) *Give unto the Lord the glory due to His name; Worship the Lord in the beauty of holiness.* I love God so much that I show Him that love by worshipping Him.

Offering: Treasures in Heaven (use Worship Power Lesson 2, slide B)

Sometimes people call our money and possessions treasures. They call them that because they are valuable. God doesn't mind us having money and possessions, but He wants us to consider Him the most valuable thing in our lives. When we do that, we'll want to give in the offering to build the Kingdom of God.

Show slide B. *Matthew 6:21 (NIV) says, "For where your treasure is, there your heart will be also."*

Have a child pray over the offering.

Skit: Tyler the Power Tool Guy's Favorite Power Tool (use Worship Power Lesson 2, slides C & D)

Supplies needed: Tyler has a portable toolbox or toolbelt with various tools and is dressed in blue jeans and a plaid shirt, etc. If you use a girl in the skit, have her dress the same and call her Tyler the Power

Tool Gal.

Tyler the Power Tool Guy: Hi, everyone. What are you learning about today?

Leader: Hello, Tyler the Power Tool Guy. We're learning that only God is worthy of our worship. Remember how I asked you to show us your favorite power tool today?

Tyler: I sure do.

Leader: It must be pretty small. I don't see it anywhere.

Tyler: Nope, it's not small. It's big. I couldn't bring it because it's too big to carry. But I did bring a picture. (Show slide C)

Leader: That tool looks complicated to use. What is it?

Tyler: It's called a lathe. It is complicated, but it does so much. I use it for shaping and cutting designs in metal and wood. It shapes, drills, sands, knurls, turns, cuts, and forms. It's hard to learn to use, but once you learn, it is a great power tool.

Leader: Are you an expert at it?

Tyler: No, I wouldn't call myself an expert, but I do a lot on the lathe. I have a picture of something I created using this tool. (Show slide D) See the design in the chair? I did that with a lathe.

Leader: That's amazing. You have a lot of talent.

Tyler: Awe, shucks. It was nothing. I couldn't have done it without my lathe. I guess you could say my lathe is a little like God.

Leader: I don't understand. A lathe is a power tool, and God is... well... God.

Tyler: True, but a lathe is my only power tool worthy of being called my favorite tool, and God is the only one worthy of my worship.

Leader: Oh, now I see what you mean.

Tyler: I have to go now. I need to clean my lathe. Bye. (Tyler exits.)

Verse of the Day: Psalm 29:2 (NKJV) *Give unto the Lord the glory due to His name; Worship the Lord in the beauty of holiness.*

Memory Verse Talk: (use Worship Power Lesson 2, slide A)

I am so happy that God gives me the opportunity to worship Him. Psalm 29:2 (NKJV) says, "Give unto the Lord the glory due to His name; Worship the Lord in the beauty of holiness." According to this verse, I worship God because He is the only one who has glory due His name. Not only that, but God is holy, and His holiness is beauty. Nobody else is holy and has glory like my God.

Memory Verse Activity: (use Worship Power Lesson 2, slide A)

Supplies needed: none

Have your students sing this memory verse. You can teach them to sing the words to a song they already know, or you can use the song, **Give Unto the Lord the Glory** by Scriptures for Kids. It can be found at this YouTube link. https://www.youtube.com/watch?v=qPHFv_PbSik

Bible Story: Moses Learns God's Name & Jesus Uses God's Name

(Exodus 3:1-15)

Supplies needed: story bag or tote bag with stuffed animal sheep, plant or picture of a bush, flash paper (optional), lighter, fake chains or picture of slave in chains, name tag with I AM written on it, name tag with YAHWEH written on it, slice of bread, flashlight, Lego block door

Preparation: Place items in a tote bag or story bag and pull them out as you're telling the story.

Did you know God has a name? A lot of people think that God's name is God, but that isn't true. He is God, but that's not His name. Some people say God's name is Jesus. That is true. God the Son is named Jesus, and His name is Holy, but God the Father isn't Jesus, and God the Holy Spirit isn't Jesus. There is one name God has that God the Father, God the Son, and God the Holy Spirit share. That's the name that has God's glory attached to it. Would you like to know what that name is? Then listen to these stories.

Show stuffed sheep. *The first story happened when Moses was tending sheep. Moses saw a bush on fire in a nearby cave.*

Show plant or picture of a bush. *The unusual thing about this bush was even though it was on fire, it didn't burn up the bush. This wasn't an ordinary fire. God was in that bush, and He is sometimes called a consuming fire.* Light flash paper (optional) or lighter.

God called out to Moses, and Moses went in the cave to get a closer look. Not only was God in the burning bush but He spoke to Moses. He told Moses to take off His shoes because this is a holy place. Show shoes or sandals. *The truth is anywhere God shows up in His glory is a holy place because God is holy.*

Moses knew that, and He hid His face because He was in awe of the beauty of God's holiness. God told him that He wanted him to go to Egypt to rescue God's people from slavery. Show fake chains or picture of slave in chains.

Moses was surprised because he didn't believe he was worthy of carrying out a mission like this, but God told him to go. He asked God who he should tell them sent him. That's when God told Moses His name. He said, I AM is sending you. Show name badge with I AM written on it.

Many of the names God uses begins with I AM. In the Hebrew language, I AM is YAHWEH, the most Holy name of God. Show name tag with YAHWEH written on it.

I AM means He is always with us. I am means He is everything we need. What we want or need God to be, He is I AM. That's a great reason to worship Him.

When Jesus came to Earth, because He is God, He used the name Jesus, but He also used the name I AM. He said, "I AM the bread of light." Show bread.

I AM the light of the world. Show flashlight.

He said, "I AM the door." Show a Lego block door.

And He said, "I AM the Way, the Truth, and the Life. Those are amazing statements. They mean that Jesus is the Holy God. In John 8:58, Jesus said, "Very truly I tell you," Jesus answered, "before Abraham was born, I AM!" So when we are worshipping Jesus, we are worshipping God.

Optional Video: That's My King

This would be a great time to show the video ***That's My King***. Your church may already own it. You can find it at Worship House or on YouTube at this link. https://youtu.be/yzqTFNfeDnE

Worship Expression: Barak (Use Worship Power Lesson 2, slide E)

The word Barak means to bow down before God. A lot of people think this means they're supposed to kneel before they pray, but it means much more. In Heaven, when Christians see Jesus, they will bow at His feet and give any rewards they've been given to Him. In Revelation 4:11, they'll say, "You are worthy, our Lord and God to receive glory and honor and power, for you created all things, and by your will they were created and have their being." It also says that at the name of Jesus, every knee shall bow. So, when we worship and behold the glory and beauty of God, we won't bow because we've been told we should. We'll bow because God is worthy of our worship.

Praise and Worship: Choose a couple of fast song and a slow song to lead children into praise and worship. It works well to talk to the children about what worship is and why it's important before you enter into this time. You can have a children's praise team, but until they understand leading praise and worship, have an adult leader or yourself be the worship leader.

Object Lesson:

1. **Object Lesson: Wow Moments**

Supplies needed: none

Have you ever had a wow moment? I have.

Tell about a time or something you saw that made you go wow. It could be seeing the Grand Canyon, Niagara Falls or a double rainbow, or your wedding day, or when you first saw your child. Allow some of your students to tell about some of their wow moments.

We've all had wow moments in our lives, and hopefully we'll have many more. But when we worship God, and He shows us His glory, that's a wow moment bigger than any other wow moment could ever be. Even the names God uses make us go wow.

Adonai means the Lord God.

Yahweh means the Great I Am.

El Shaddai means God Almighty.

El Roi means the God who sees me.

Elohim is Father God or God the Creator of everything.

Yahweh Yireh means I AM your Provider.

Yahweh Ropheka means I AM your Healer.

Yahweh Nissi I AM your banner.

Yahweh Shalom means I AM your Peace.

Yahweh Tsuri means I AM your Rock.

El Olam means The Eternal God.

Yeshua means Jesus, the Son of God.

Can we all say Wow together? Wow.

2. Object Lesson: Magnify the Lord

Supplies needed: magnifying glass or binoculars

Allow each student to look through the magnifying glass.

What happens when you look through this magnifying glass (binoculars). Allow the students to answer.

In a way, worship works in the same way. God appears bigger when we worship Him. That's why King David said in Psalm 34:3 (NKJV), "Oh, magnify the Lord with me, And let us exalt His name together." King David wanted to worship God and His Name, so God would appear bigger to him.

When we looked at the objects through the magnifying glass (binoculars), all the items appeared bigger. Were they really bigger? Allow the students to answer.

That's the difference between worship and a magnifier. God is bigger and more spectacular than we could ever understand or know. When we worship, He appears bigger to us, but He is much bigger and greater than He ever appears to us.

Message: Spiritual Act of Worship (Use Worship Power Lesson 2, slide F)

Supplies needed: jar or glass, pebbles, sand, pitcher of water

Show slide E. *Romans 12:1 says, "Therefore, I urge you, brothers and sisters, in view of God's mercy, to offer your bodies as a living sacrifice, holy and pleasing to God—this is your true and proper worship."*

This isn't just a one-time thing where we get saved and give our lives to God. God wants us to continually give more of our lives to Him. It's a lifetime act of worship.

Show jar. *This jar represents giving our lives to God. Is this jar full?* Allow students to answer. If nobody mentions it, point out that the jar is full of air. *We give our lives to God when we get saved, but there's so much more we can give than just air.*

Pour pebbles into the jar. *We can go to church and read our Bible. We can tell God we love Him, and begin to worship Him in church. Now, is the jar full? It's full, but there's still more we can give.*

Pour sand into the jar. *We can start living our lives for God. We can tell our friends about Jesus and show love to others. Is the jar full now? There's still more we can give.*

Pour water into the jar. *When we sacrifice our lives to God, there's always more we can give to Him, but everything we give in worship is rewarded with a satisfying life. Is the jar full now?* Allow students to answer.

Yes, the jar is full, but there's still more. If you took a microscope and looked at the molecules in this jar, you would see there's still more room. There's always more of our lives we can give.

Response Time and Worship Expression: Barak (Use Worship Power Lesson 2, slide E)

The word Barak means to bow down before God. A lot of people think this means they're supposed to kneel before they pray, but it means much more. In Heaven, when Christians see Jesus, they will bow at His feet and give any rewards they've been given to Him. We will give Him everything. In Revelation 4:11, they'll say, "You are worthy, our Lord and God to receive glory and honor and power, for you created all things, and by your will they were created and have their being." It also says that at the name of Jesus, every knee shall bow. So, when we worship and behold the glory and beauty of God, we won't bow because we've been told we should. We'll bow because God is worthy of our worship.

Let's take some time to worship. If you want to bow down you can. Let the students know you will be laying a hand on their heads and praying for them like you did last week. This time, pray they give more of themselves in worship.

Small Group Activity: Worship Expression Zamar

Supplies needed: kid's instruments (You can make these from common household items if the church doesn't have kid's instruments. Check online for how to make them. If you have time, you might even allow the students to make the instruments.)

Zamar means to worship God joyfully with musical instruments, so we're going to take some time to play these instruments. You don't have to play them well, but I'd like you to play them joyfully.

Lesson 3 - Worship In Spirit and In Truth

Focus Point: God wants us to worship in spirit and in truth.

Goal: Students will learn what it means to worship Him in spirit and in truth.

Verse of the Day: John 4:24 (NKJV) *God is Spirit, and those who worship Him must worship in spirit and truth.*

Supplies Needed:

- doctor puppet or doctor costume for skit
- portable toolbox with various tools
- Tyler the Power Tool Guy Skit: Tyler wears a portable toolbox or toolbelt with various tools and is dressed in blue jeans and a plaid shirt, etc.
- engraved wood project (optional)
- bouncing ball
- bottle of water
- pitcher of water
- lotta bowl (optional object you can find online or in a magic shop)
- cup
- Styrofoam cup with holes punch in the bottom
- bowl or tray
- small table
- a few unbreakable items to set on table

Opening: *Power Tools Countdown* (optional) or *Power Tools* Slide

Welcome:

Welcome children. God wants us to worship Him in spirit and in truth. We'll learn what that means today, but let's start this service with some praise and worship. For five minutes, let's tell worship God and tell Him how worthy He is. You can shout Hallelujah or say you're worthy, or even I love you, Jesus.

Tell the students when to start. If your students are not ready for five minutes, start them out at one minute, and build from there.

Prayer: Ask a child to pray over the service.

Rules: (use rules slide) Go over the 5 Ups Rules.

Go over the *5 Ups Rules*: 1. Sit up straight. 2. Listen up. 3. Hush up. 4. Don't get up and run around or go to the bathroom. 5. Worship Up! (stand up and participate during praise and worship)

Theme or Activity Songs: Choose one of two fast moving activity or theme songs that go with the curriculum.

Game Time: Jesus Says Worship (use game time slide)

Supplies needed: none

This is played the same way as Simon Says, only you say Jesus says. Say various things children might do to worship God. Some suggestions are stomp your feet, jump up and down, sing, kneel, clap your hands, raise your hands, lay on the floor, spin around, dance, etc.

Memory Verse Skit: (use Worship Power Lesson 3, slide A)

Supplies needed: doctor puppet or doctor costume for skit

Doctor Word: Hi kids. I'm Doctor Word. I'm called that because I'm a doctor and because I love the Word of God. There are certain procedures I must follow as a doctor licensed by the state. For instance, I can't tell anyone about a patient's health unless that patient gives me permission. And there are certain drugs I can only prescribe if I document why the patient needs them. When I perform surgery, there are policies for making sure I have a sterile surgical room. I also must wash my hands a certain way and wear gloves, a mask, a hair cover, and a surgical gown. There are good reasons for each of these policies, and I always make sure I follow them. To not do so could end in disaster for the patient and for me.

There are also policies you should follow to worship God. Some people think those policies include how you worship. Do you raise your hands or fall down? Do you laugh or cry? Do you shout or be very quiet? But God doesn't care how you worship. All of those ways to worship are pleasing to Him if you follow His worship policy. It's easy to remember because it's our memory verse for today. John 4:24 (NKJV) says, *"God is Spirit, and those who worship Him must worship in spirit and truth."* The spirit part means we worship from our whole heart and surrender to what the Holy Spirit wants to do. The truth part means we always worship according to Scripture. We never try to worship doing something that Scripture tells us not to do. For instance, we would never use icons or special crystals to help us worship. I have to go now. Remember to worship in spirit and in truth.

Offering: Giving to Be Blessed

Giving is an act of worship. Just like in worship, when we give with our heart out of love for God, God will bless us and be pleased with our offering, but if we give because we have to, that doesn't honor God or make Him happy with our giving. We want to give in the right way, as an act of worship. That's when it's more blessed to give than to receive.

Skit: Tyler the Power Tool Guy Makes a Project

Supplies Needed: Tyler has a portable toolbox or toolbelt with various tools and is dressed in blue jeans and a plaid shirt, etc. If you use a girl in the skit, have her dress the same and call her Tyler the Power Tool Gal. If you have a woodworker in your church, use one of his creations as an object lesson. Change the script accordingly. If not, use Worship Power Lesson 3, slide B.

Tyler the Power Tool Guy: Hi there. Today, I wanted to show you something I made with my lathe power tool. I'm very proud of it.

Leader: I'd love to see it.

Tyler: It's still at my woodshop, but I have a picture of it.

(Show slide B)

Leader: That's beautiful. What is it?

Tyler: It's the lid for a chest I'm making. I'm pretty proud of it.

Leader: That's amazing. Did you do all of that engraving with your lathe?

Tyler: Not all of it. I used a power saw and a jigsaw for parts of it, and I had to hand carve to more delicate parts, but without my lathe, it would have taken a lot longer to make.

Leader: It's obvious you put a lot of time and effort into making this.

Tyler: I did. It's a gift for someone very special. I wanted to let this person know how much I care.

Leader: That's a little bit like what I'm teaching about today..

Tyler: I don't understand. Your teaching about woodworking in church?

Leader: No, not that. I'm teaching about worshipping God in spirit and in truth. Worship is expressing our love for God. You are expressing your love for this special person in your woodworking. Just as we should express our worship in spirit and in truth, your expressing yourself with you skill and passion.

Tyler: Don't forget my power tools.

Leader: That's right. And your power tools.

Tyler: That makes a lot of sense, but I need to go put the finishing touches on this chest lid now. Good-bye.

(Exits)

Verse of the Day: John 4:24 (NKJV) *God is Spirit, and those who worship Him must worship in spirit and truth.*

Memory Verse Talk: (use Worship Power Lesson 3, slide A)

Supplies needed: None

John 4:24 (NKJV) says, "God is Spirit, and those who worship Him must worship in spirit and truth." Worship isn't about what we see on the outside. While people who are worshipping God might jump up and down, shout, sing, cry, and laugh, that isn't worship. If we are truly worshipping, that's only the expressions of our worship. True worship happens in the heart. When we surrender our lives to the Holy Spirit and we trust His Word, the Bible, then we are worshipping in spirit and in truth.

Memory Verse Activity: Bouncing Ball

Supplies needed: bouncing ball

Have your students stand in a circle. When the ball is bounced to a student, that student must say the next word in the verse. Repeat several times until everyone has had a turn.

Bible Story: The Woman at the Well

(Use Worship Power Lesson 3 slides B - D)

(John 4:4-26)

Supplies needed: bottle of water, Worship Power Lesson 3, slides B through D

I'm really thirsty. I've been thirsty all morning. Excuse me while I have a drink of water. Drink water from the water bottle and tell your students how it really quenched your thirsty.

Today, I'm going to tell you the story of a time when Jesus was thirsty. He was in a place called Samaria, and He sat down at a well.

Show slide B. *Now, we go to the store and buy water bottles to take with us on long walks, but back then, they didn't have water bottles. When you were thirsty, you had to find a well and lower a pail or a cup into the well to get some water. I'm glad we don't have to do that every time we want to take a long walk.*

Jesus sat at the well around noon, the hottest time of day. He was so thirsty, but he didn't have a cup or a pail to lower into the well. I bet you were thinking, "Why doesn't he just invent a water bottle or created a cup out of thin air." He could have done that. He could have even made a wooden cup since He was a carpenter, but Jesus had other plans.

Show slide C. *Just then, a woman walked up to the well carrying water jugs. She wasn't just any woman. She was a Samaritan woman. Jews in those days thought Samaritans weren't even worthy of talking to, but Jesus doesn't have any prejudices like that. He created everyone to be of equal worth. He spoke to the Samaritan woman and asked her for a drink of water. The Samaritan woman was surprised that a Jew would talk to her, let alone ask her for a drink. Jews just didn't do that.*

When the Samaritan woman asked why He asked her for a drink, Jesus told her if she knew who He was, she would ask Him for a drink. Then He said that He had living water. Whoever drank from the water He had would never thirst again. She didn't know this, but Jesus was talking about the living water God gives us when we get saved. It satisfies our soul like nothing can. Jesus surprised her again and told her about her life and the wrong things she'd done. He was letting her know that the life she was living away from God would never satisfy her.

The woman knew Jesus must be special. She believed He was a prophet, but she was confused about worship and wanted to know where people should worship. The Samaritans worshipped on a mountain, and the Jews worshipped in the temple in Jerusalem.

Jesus told her it didn't matter where she worshipped. The important thing was how she worshipped.

Show slide D. *In John 4: 23-24 (NKJV), Jesus said, "Yet a time is coming and has now come when the true worshipers will worship the Father in the Spirit and in truth, for they are the kind of worshipers the Father seeks. God is spirit, and his worshipers must worship in the Spirit and in truth."*

God doesn't care where we worship or how we express our worship. God cares about what is in our hearts. He wants us to worship Him in Spirit and in Truth.

Worship Expression: Yadah (Use Worship Power Lesson 3, slides E & F)

Show slide E. *Our praise word for today is Yadah. It means to raise our hand to God. It is a sign of surrender and adoration.*

Show slide F. *The word is used in Psalm 63:1-4. "You, God, are my God, earnestly I seek you; I thirst for you, my whole being longs for you, in a dry and parched land where there is no water. I have seen you in the sanctuary and beheld your power and your glory. Because your love is better than life, my lips will glorify you. I will praise you as long as I live, and in your name I will YADAH lift up my hands."*

So let's Yadah today as we worship.

Praise and Worship: Choose a couple of fast song and a slow song to lead children into praise and worship. It works well to talk to the children about what worship is and why it's important before you enter into this time. You can have a children's praise team, but until they understand leading praise and worship, have an adult leader or yourself be the worship leader.

Object Lessons:

1. Living Water and Broken Wells

Supplies needed: pitcher of water, lotta bowl (optional object you can find online or in a magic shop), cup, Styrofoam cup with holes punch in the bottom, bowl or tray to catch excess water

As you are reading the following paragraph to your students, fill a cup with water until it overflows. If you are using a lotta bowl, have it filled completely before the service, and pour out water from time to time throughout the lesson saying, *God's living water never runs dry.* The lotta bowl will appear as if it has an endless supply of water.

In Jeremiah 2:13, God corrected His people for committing two sins. The first was forsaking God who He called the spring of living water, and the second was going to broken wells that couldn't hold any water. I have here a pitcher of water (lotta bowl). When we love and worship God. He fills us to overflowing. We never run out of His living water. The Holy Spirit fills us and satisfies us with His joy and peace like springs of living water.

As you read the next paragraph, pour water into the Styrofoam cup. It should leak our of the holes you've punched in the bottom.

But God also said that His people were using broken wells that hold no water. That is what happens when your worship is just a duty you feel like you have to do and you don't worship in spirit and in truth. Anything you love more than God becomes like a broken well. It can never satisfy your thirst. There are lots of things we can do that aren't a sin, but if we put them before God, they become like broken wells. Can you name a few things people put before God? Allow the students to answer.

How do we get this living water? Jesus is the living water. In John 7:38 (NIV), Jesus says, "Whoever believes in me, as Scripture has said, rivers of living water will flow from within them."

2. Vain Worship

(Matthew 21:12-13; Mark 11:15-18)

Supplies needed: small table with unbreakable items.

Knock over the table. Let the students know you did this to show an object lesson and not because you were angry. Ask them if they were surprised you did that. Ask them how they would feel if Jesus came into church next week and knock over the tables.

This happened in the Bible. The worship in the temple was so displeasing to God that Jesus went into the temple, knocked over the tables, and drove people out with a whip. Wow. He must have been really angry. He told them why He was so angry about their worship. Here are two kinds of worship God doesn't like.

Hypocritical Worship: Jesus doesn't like worship that is only lip service. If you pretend to worship God with your words, but you don't love God, it isn't true worship. God wants us to worship from the heart. This is worshipping with our spirit. Mark 7:6.

False Worship: Jesus told the people they were following a bunch of rules about worshipping God that weren't even in the Bible. When you try to worship, but you don't believe what the Bible says, it is false worship. God wants us to know Him by studying His Word. Then we will worship Him in truth. Matthew 15:9.

God is pleased with our worship when we worship Him in Spirit and in truth.

Message: The Kind of Worship that Pleases God

Supplies needed: none

Just as there are kind of worship that God hates, there is worship that pleases God.

Worship in spirit and in truth. We know about this worship from our memory verse and Bible story. John 4:24 (NKJV) God is Spirit, and those who worship Him must worship in spirit and truth.

Worship from a pure heart and clean hands. Psalm 24:3-4 (NIV) Who may ascend the mountain of the Lord? Who may stand in his holy place? The one who has clean hands and a pure heart, who does not trust in an idol or swear by a false god. To have a pure heart, we accept Jesus as our Savior. To have clean hands, we do what's right and ask God to forgive us when we fail.

Worship in faith. Hebrews 11:6 (NIV) says, "And without faith it is impossible to please God, because anyone who comes to him must believe that he exists and that he rewards those who earnestly seek him." When we believe in God, seek Him, and know He will reward us with His joy and peace, then we worship the way God wants.

Worship Expression and Response Time: Hallal (Use Worship Power Lesson 3, slide G & H)

The word, Hallal, is the main word for praise. It's the word that makes the word hallelujah. It means to be clear, to praise, to shine, to boast, show, to rave, celebrate, to be clamorously foolish. In other words, it means to joyfully celebrate God.

Show slide G. *HALLAL is a primary Hebrew root word for praise. Our word "hallelujah" comes from this base word. It's used in Psalm 150. I want you all to repeat the words in a joyful way to celebrate the Lord. You can even shout the words if you want.*

Show Slide H. *Psalm 150 Praise the Lord. Praise God in his sanctuary; praise him in his mighty heavens.*

Praise him for his acts of power; praise him for his surpassing greatness.

Praise him with the sounding of the trumpet, praise him with the harp and lyre,

Praise him with timbrel and dancing, praise him with the strings and pipe,

Praise him with the clash of cymbals, praise him with resounding cymbals.

Let everything that has breath praise the Lord. Praise the Lord.

Have the students spend some time celebrating and worshipping God. Let the students know you will be laying a hand on their heads and praying for them like you did last week. After worship time, ask them what happened or what they felt during worship time.

Small Group Activity and Worship Expression: Praise Ye the Lord

Supplies needed: none

This is a classic children's ministry song. If you've never heard it, you can find it on YouTube at this link. https://www.youtube.com/watch?v=p8OylXvM384 The music is a bit dorky, so I recommend you don't use it unless you find a more modernized version. Divide the students into two teams. One team sings Hallelu, Hallelujah. The other team sings Praise Ye the Lord. Then you can alternate. The loudest team wins.

Show slide L. *There is one more praise and worship word I want to teach you today. The word is Shabach. Shabach means to shout praises to God, so when we sing this next song, we're going to shout praises to God.* Instruct the students how to sing this game.

Lesson 4 – Enjoying Worship

Focus Point: Worship enjoying God.

Goal: Students will learn God wants them to enjoy Him through worship.

Verse of the Day: Psalm 16:11 (NKJV) *You will show me the path of life; In Your presence is fullness of joy. At Your right hand are pleasures forevermore.*

Supplies Needed:

- doctor puppet or doctor costume for skit
- portable toolbox with various tools
- Tyler the Power Tool Guy Skit: Tyler wears a portable toolbox or toolbelt with various tools and is dressed in blue jeans and a plaid shirt, etc.
- Snickers bar
- balloon filled halfway with water
- candle
- lighter
- bottle of bubbles

Opening: *Power Tools Countdown* (optional) or *Power Tools* Slide

Welcome: Prayer Time

Welcome. For the last three weeks, we've been learning about the power of worship. Today we're going to talk about how God wants us to have fun worshipping Him. For five minutes, let's enjoy God by worshipping Him. You can shout Hallelujah or say you're worthy, or even I love you, Jesus.

Tell the students when to start. If your students are not ready for five minutes, start them out at one minute, and build from there.

Prayer: Ask a child to pray over the service.

Rules: (use rules slide) Go over the 5 Ups Rules.

Go over the *5 Ups Rules*: 1. Sit up straight. 2. Listen up. 3. Hush up. 4. Don't get up and run around or go to the bathroom. 5. Worship Up! (stand up and participate during praise and worship)

Theme or Activity Songs: Choose one of two fast moving activity or theme songs that go with the curriculum.

Game Time: Dance Contest (use game time slide)

Supplies Needed: none

For this game, you can choose a certain number of students or have every student participate. If you have every student participate, choose someone to judge the contest. If only a certain number of students participate, then have the other students judge the contest by clapping for each student participating. The goal of the contest is to have each student dance to upbeat music. When the game ends, tell the students how King David danced before the Lord as an expression of worship.

Memory Verse Skit: (use Worship Power Lesson 4, slide A)

Supplies needed: doctor puppet or doctor costume for skit

Doctor Word: Hi kids. I'm Doctor Word. I'm called that because I'm a doctor and because I love the Word of God. I love being a doctor. Helping people get better when they are sick is a joy I can't describe. But it doesn't even compare to the joy that comes from worshipping God and being in His presence. Psalm 16:11 (NKJV) says, *"You will show me the path of life; In Your presence is fullness of joy; At Your right hand are pleasures forevermore."* Let's enjoy God today.

Offering: Joyful Giving

Did you know God wants us to be happy when we give in the offering? 2 Corinthians 9:6 (NKJV) says, "God loves a cheerful giver." So, let's all cheer before we give today. Encourage children to clap and shout, "Praise the Lord."

Skit: Tyler the Power Tool Guy

Supplies Needed: Tyler has a portable toolbox or toolbelt with various tools and is dressed in blue jeans and a plaid shirt, etc. If you use a girl in the skit, have her dress the same and call her Tyler the Power Tool Gal.

Tyler the Power Tool Guy: (Comes in) Hi everyone. I can't stay long today.

Leader: I'm sorry to hear that, Tyler. I was hoping you'd tell us some more about your lathe and wooden chest.

Tyler: I wish I could, but the boss had me working overtime so much this week that I didn't have time to work on my project.

Leader: Why so much overtime?

Tyler: We have a new job. Someone bought a fixer upper house and hired us to fix it up.

Leader: That sounds like fun.

Tyler: It can be, but I enjoy making things so much more than fixing something that's broken. That's sort of how I feel about this house. I like fixing it up, but I really enjoy making things like that chest. I have to go now. Bye, everyone.

(Exits)

Verse of the Day: Psalm 16:11 (NKJV) *You will show me the path of life; In Your presence is fullness of joy; At Your right hand are pleasures forevermore.*

Memory Verse Talk: (use Worship Power Lesson 4, slide A)

Supplies needed: none

Psalm 16:11 (NKJV) says, "You will show me the path of life; In Your presence is fullness of joy; At Your right hand are pleasures forevermore." Let's look at this verse for a moment. Jesus said, "I am the way, the truth, and the life," so God shows us the path of life, and that path is in Jesus. That should make us happy since all we have to do is give our lives to Him, and He'll guide us every step of the way.

We've been talking about worship the last few weeks and how worship brings us into the manifest presence of God. In God's presence is fullness of joy. At His right hand are pleasures forever.

Have you ever heard someone say they don't want to follow God because they want to have fun? Those people don't understand that we are the one's having fun. God wants to fill us up with His joy. Some Christians believe that they have to be sad and serious when they're worshipping God. I hope you realize by now that God wants to fill us with joy. He doesn't want us to be sad in His presence. He wants us to shout, and cheer, and laugh, and dance.

Memory Verse Activity: Say It with Motions

Divide the class into teams of four to six students each. Try to include a couple of older students in each team. The teams have five minutes to come up with motions to act out for the memory verse. Give each team a chance to show their motions.

Bible Story: David Danced

(2 Samuel 6:12-19)

Supplies Needed: none

Tell your students to listen to this story carefully. Whenever you say dance, they are to get up and leap, dance, or spin. Whenever you say sad, they are to cry boo hoo, boo hoo.

*Have you ever had something so exciting happen that you wanted to leap up and down, dance, and spin? When we are **happy**, we sometimes feel like doing just that. This story is about King David. King David was called a man after God's own heart. He was called that because, even though he made mistakes that made God **sad**, He loved to worship God. It made him **happy**.*

*(Show slide B) This is the Ark of the Covenant. In King David's time, it was how God showed His manifest presence and glory to His people. King David wanted the ark to be in Jerusalem, his capital city, so God's presence would always be close to him. He tried to move the ark once before, but he did it the wrong way, and it ended in tragedy. David left the ark in a tent miles away for the city. It made him **sad** the ark wasn't near him.*

*One day, David decided he would move the ark to his city. He studied God's Word to make sure He moved the ark the right way this time. As the men carried the ark into the city, David was so **happy**. He had musicians play, trumpets blast, and singers sing. Some people were so **happy** they started shouting praises to God. Before long, David became so **happy**, he removed his outer coat and danced before the Lord with all his might. This made God very **happy**.*

*With all the praises, worship, and dancing going on to worship the Lord, you would think it would make everyone **happy** that the Ark of the Covenant, God's presence, was coming into Jerusalem, but it didn't. David's wife was angry. She thought dancing, shouting, and singing before the Lord was undignified. This made David **sad** and angry. He told her he would become even more undignified worshipping God. Worshipping God made him **happy**, and he wasn't going to let anyone stop his worship.*

Worship Expression: Machowl (Use Worship Power Lesson 4, slide B)

Machowl means to worship God by dancing or spinning about. It's the way David expressed his worship to God when he danced. It's found in Psalm 149:3 (NIV). Let them praise his name with dancing and make music to him with timbrel and harp.

It's now time for praise and worship. Let's praise God today by spinning around or dancing. For praise and worship, choose songs the students can dance to.

Praise and Worship: Choose a couple of fast song and a slow song to lead children into praise and worship. It works well to talk to the children about what worship is and why it's important before you enter into this time. You can have a children's praise team, but until they understand leading praise and worship, have an adult leader or yourself be the worship leader.

Object Lessons:

1. God Satisfies

Supplies needed: Snickers bar

If you have snack time, consider serving Snickers bite size candy bars. Have an alternate for students allergic to nuts.

Snickers used to have an advertising slogan that said, "Snickers really satisfies you." While it's nice to think that a sugary chocolate candy bar can satisfy your hunger, it doesn't. What it really does is make you hungry for more sugary treats.

Worshipping God is not like a Snickers bar. God satisfies us like nothing can. Psalm 107:9 (NASB) says, "For He has satisfied the thirsty soul." When we worship and enjoy the Lord, He will satisfy us. Now, that's a slogan I can get behind.

2. Joy in the Flame

Supplies needed: balloon filled halfway with water, candle, lighter

Preparation: Fill the balloon halfway with water, and light the candle.

Today, we are talking about enjoying God in worship. Some people wonder how you can have the joy of the Lord, when things are going wrong. There may be a sickness in your family, or your parents might be fighting or getting a divorce. You might have had a fight with your best friend, or a bully might be picking on you at school. How can you have joy when things like that are happening?

There are many people in the Bible who went through hard times. Paul was imprisoned and beaten. Peter was thrown in prison more than once. And John was boiled in oil. When they couldn't kill

John, they banished him to a remote island. Even so, none of these disciples lost their joy. That's because the joy of the Lord is a supernatural joy given by the Holy Spirit. It means God is larger than your problems, so you are satisfied in Him. When you worship, God gives you that kind of joy. The more you worship, the larger God becomes in your life. He gives you joy that can't be quenched by any flame of difficulty.

Show balloon and light candle. *Pretend this balloon is a Christian. He's been worshipping, and he has the joy of the Holy Spirit inside him. After he leaves church, he might have something bad happen to him.*

Place the balloon over the fire. Make sure you place the balloon so the part with water is touching the flames. You may want to practice this before the service.

Even though trials come, if we are worshipping and the Holy Spirit lives inside of us, the flames of those trials won't destroy us. It's all right to feel sad when bad things happen, but when we worship Jesus even though we are sad, it's possible to be joyful and sad at the same time.

Optional Video: Joy is Contagious

Sometimes it's easier for children to get this concept if they see it. Here are a few videos on YouTube you might want to show your students. These videos are long, so I suggest you only show a few minutes of one or two of them.

https://youtu.be/IBiwQhbyfkk

https://youtu.be/SyiqPQ4ZY6c

https://youtu.be/L88V4qAtUDU

Message: It's Bubbling (Use Worship Power Lesson 4, slide C, D, E)

Supplies needed: bottle of bubbles

Start making bubbles and continue throughout the object lesson. *I bet you wonder why I have this bottle of bubbles. I'm using these bubbles to illustrate how God wants to fill you with so much joy that it bubbles out of you.*

Romans 15:13 (NKJV) says, "Now may the God of hope fill you with all joy and peace in believing, that you may abound (bubble up) in hope by the power of the Holy Spirit."

John 4:14 (NKJV) says, "But whoever drinks of the water that I shall give him will never thirst. But the water that I shall give him will become in him a fountain of water springing (bubbling) up into everlasting life."

1 Peter 1:8 (NIV) says, "Though you have not seen him, you love him; and even though you do not see him now, you believe in him and are filled (bubbling up) with an inexpressible and glorious joy.

One thing all these verses show us is that when we are worshipping God, He wants to fill us with joy until it bubbles up inside. When joy fills you and bubbles us inside of you, sometimes it will cause you to smile, and sometimes it will even cause you to laugh. God loves us and wants us to enjoy worshipping

Him.

Response Time:

For response time, have the students spend some time celebrating and worshipping God. Let the students know you will be laying a hand on their heads and praying for them to be filled with joy. Tell them to expect God to fill them with joy, and sometimes laughter. After worship time, ask them what happened or what they felt during worship time.

Small Group Activity: Bubbling

Supplies needed: bubbles for everyone

Have the students spend time playing with bubbles. Take this outside if possible. One way to save money and make great bubbles is to use a bowl of dishwashing liquid mixed with a little cornstarch. Then buy a wand for each student to dip into the solution.

About the Author

Pastor Tamera Kraft has been a children's pastor for over thirty years. She is the director of a ministry called Revival Fire For Kids where she mentors other children's leaders, teaches workshops, and is a children's ministry consultant and children's revivalist. She is a recipient of the 2007 National Children's Leaders Association Shepherd's Cup for lifetime achievement in children's ministry.

You can find out more about Revival Fire for Kids at http://revivalfire4kids.net.